Inspiration

from

POPE FRANCIS

Inspiration

from

POPE FRANCIS

By Jorge Mario Bergoglio
Pope Francis

Compiled by
María Gabriela Flores, FSP

Pauline
BOOKS & MEDIA
Boston

Library of Congress Cataloging-in-Publication Data

Francis, Pope, 1936-
  [Palabras del Papa Francisco. English]
  Inspiration from Pope Francis / by Jorge Mario Bergoglio, Pope Francis ; compiled by
María Gabriela Flores, FSP.
     pages cm
  ISBN-13: 978-0-8198-3722-6
  ISBN-10: 0-8198-3722-9
  1. Catholic Church--Sermons. I. Flores, María Gabriela, editor of compilation. II. Title.
  BX1378.7.F745 2014
  252'.02--dc23

                              2013039113

Cover design by Rosana Usselmann

Cover photo: *L'Osservatore Romano* photo service

Originally published in Spanish as *Palabras del Papa Francisco* by the Association of the
Daughters of St. Paul Argentina (Paulinas), Buenos Aires, Argentina, copyright © 2013.

Translated by Marlyn Monge, FSP

Copyright © Association of the Daughters of St. Paul Argentina and
Maria Gabriela Flores, FSP

Published by Pauline Books & Media, 50 Saint Pauls Avenue, Boston, MA 02130-3491.
www.pauline.org

Printed in the U.S.A.

Pauline Books & Media is the publishing house of the Daughters of St. Paul, an
international congregation of women religious serving the Church with the com-
munications media.

1 2 3 4 5 6 7 8 9   18 17 16 15 14

CONTENTS

INTRODUCTION

Jorge Mario Bergoglio, now Pope Francis, was born in Argentina on December 17, 1936, in the Flores neighborhood of Buenos Aires. From his youth he felt called to be a priest, and, after working as a chemical technician, he entered the seminary of Devoto. In 1958 he transferred to the novitiate of the Society of Jesus and studied theology at Saint Joseph seminary. Ordained a priest in 1969, he was elected provincial superior of the Jesuits in 1973 at the young age of thirty-six. He exercised this charge during the very difficult time of Argentina's military dictatorship. After having served as provincial superior, he was the rector of *Colegio Maximo* from 1980 to 1986. Within a few years of his appointment as spiritual director in Córdoba, in 1992 Pope John Paul II named him an auxiliary bishop for the Archdiocese of Buenos Aires. After the death of Archbishop Antonio Quarracino, Bergoglio became the archbishop of Buenos Aires in 1998, and in 2001 he was named cardinal.

On March 13, 2013, Cardinal Archbishop Jorge Mario Bergoglio made history when he was elected pope. He became the first pope from the Americas, the first Spanish-speaking pope, and the first pope to choose the name Francis. When he walked out onto the balcony of Saint Peter's Basilica, he asked the faithful gathered there and those watching on television and the Internet to pray and ask for God's blessing on the Bishop of Rome. This gesture of a pope humbly bowing before the crowds, transmitted all over the world, has characterized the pontificate of Pope Francis.

This same sense of humility and closeness to the people he serves can also be found in the homilies and messages he gave as Archbishop and Cardinal of Buenos Aires. His words emphasize his care for children and the elderly; his concern for the most fragile: *cartoneros*,[*] the homeless, etc.; the high value he places on the pastoral work of priests, catechists, and pastoral ministers. He also challenged the laity and consecrated persons—in other words the whole Church—to come out of their parish settings and be a living presence in society.

---

[*] Street people who look in the garbage for paper and cardboard to sell. —Trans.

Cardinal Bergoglio didn't just speak or preach; he lived what he taught. He is an example of a priest in touch with his flock. He was known for getting around town via public transportation, speaking *with* people and not simply *to* them, and supporting the clergy in every slum and shanty village. And he would humbly beg everyone he met, "Please, I ask you to pray for me."

The thoughts that appear in this book are mainly taken from texts and homilies from 1999 to 2010. A few of his words given as pope are also included. We hope that these words will be a door through which you can enter the mind and heart of Pope Francis. We also pray that by reflecting on and praying with his words, you may be inspired to transform his thoughts into concrete actions that will serve as a path to bring you closer to Jesus Christ.

ADORATION

Because adoration is prostration, it humbly recognizes the infinite greatness of God. Only true humility can recognize true greatness while also recognizing the littleness that tries to be great. Perhaps one of the greatest evils of our time is that many adore the human and neglect the divine.

To adore is to look with trust at him who appears trustworthy because he is the giver of life, an instrument of peace, the one who brings about encounters and solidarity.

To adore is to stand before all that is not adorable, because adoration makes us free and changes us into people full of life.

To adore is not to empty but to fill one's self; to adore is to recognize and to enter into communion with Love. No one adores what he or she does not love; you do not adore the one whom you do not consider your beloved. We are loved! We are wanted! "God is Love." This certainty brings us to adore with all our heart him who loved us first (see 1 Jn 4:10).

To adore is to discover the tenderness of God; it is to find consolation and rest in his presence. To adore is to experience Psalm 23: "Even though I walk through the darkest valley, I fear no evil; for you are with me. . . . Surely goodness and mercy shall follow me all the days of my life" (Ps 23:4, 6).

To adore is to be joyful witnesses to Christ's victory and not to allow ourselves to be conquered by great tribulation. To adore is to joyfully anticipate the feast when we will meet the Shepherd, the only one worthy of adoration, who will dry all our tears and in whom we celebrate the triumph of life and love over death and hopelessness (see Rev 21–22).

To adore is to draw closer to unity, to discover ourselves as sons and daughters of the same Father, members of one family. As Saint Francis discovered, to adore is to sing praise in union with all creation and with all humanity. It is to repair the bonds that we have broken with our earth, with our brothers and sisters, and to recognize God as Lord of all things, as the good Father of the whole world.

To adore is to say "God" and to say "life." It is to find ourselves in our daily life face to face with the God of life, to adore him through our life and witness. It is to know that we have a faithful God who has stayed with us and who trusts us.

To adore is to say AMEN!

BEATITUDES

Jesus looks deep into the heart of each one of us, who come burdened with our worries and weighed down by work-related problems, and he says to us:

Blessed are you who are here in line asking
  for bread and work.

Blessed are you who have a humble heart, and
  who neither feel yourself to be greater

nor less than your brother and sister at
your side.

Blessed are you who can be proud of not
having any privilege except that of being
my beloved child.

Blessed are you who have that righteous anger
that is a hunger and thirst for justice. You
know how to complain and protest, but
without harming anyone; and you come
first of all to ask your God and Lord.

Blessed are you who do good and, despite
being misunderstood and criticized so
often, don't lower your hope-filled arms.

Blessed are you who know how to cry with
meekness and how to hope only in God.

Blessed are you not because of what you
don't have, nor because all your sufferings
will now be resolved (there is always

some suffering), but because the gift of God is so great that you can receive it only if your heart is immeasurably open. That is why Jesus calls blessed those who experience things that open and widen the heart.

We can say that when Jesus draws closer to our pain, we see things differently: Jesus speaks to us of the poor, the hungry, those who cry, those who are unjustly persecuted . . . but there is hope in the tone of his voice, so that even hearing it consoles us. Blessed are you who cry now, because you will be consoled, he tells us. And that word is like he himself wiping away our tears.

Blessed are they who have not seen and have believed: this is the beatitude of faith! In every time and in every place blessed are those who, through the Word of God—proclaimed in the

Church and witnessed by Christians—believe that Jesus Christ is the incarnate love of God, mercy incarnate. And this makes everything worth it for each one of us!

BENEDICT XVI

With great affection and profound gratitude I think about my venerated predecessor, Pope Benedict XVI. During the years of his papacy, he has enriched and strengthened the Church with his <u>magisterium,</u> his goodness, his direction, his faith, his humility, and his gentleness.

Benedict XVI has lit a flame in the depths of our hearts. This flame will continue to burn because it will be nourished by his prayer, a prayer that will still sustain the Church in its spiritual and missionary path.

BLESSING

"To bless" is composed of two words: "good" (*bien*) and "to speak" (*decir*): to speak good to the other. Blessing is Word and it is Gift. It is to speak good, giving the truth—the two together. A blessing does not consist only of "beautiful words." It is a word spoken with love, at times given with a laying of hands on one's head, or marking one's forehead with a cross, giving a good. Blessing transforms things and opens our eyes to the profound sense they contain: when one blesses the bread we become aware that it is not just a product to consume. It is the fruit of the work that is shared with familial love, as much at the kitchen or dining room table as at the table of the altar, when the bread is changed into the Body of Christ.

To offer blessings to one another is something we lack in our life as community, that is, to speak well of the good things that we give to one another. To communicate things badly to one another in public is perhaps one of our greatest defects. In the more personal contexts of friendship or family, we usually have a good discussion. However, public dialogue is difficult for us: to say things positively to one another as an institution, in front of others, for the good of others.

THE BREAD
OF HEAVEN

Remember that the Bread of Heaven is a living bread that speaks to you of planting and harvesting, because it is bread of a life that must die in order to nourish.

Remember that the Bread of Heaven is a daily bread, because your future is in the hands of our good Father and not only in human hands.

Remember that the Bread of Heaven is a bread of solidarity that one doesn't hoard for oneself, but shares and celebrates with family.

Remember that the Bread of Heaven is a bread of eternal life and not perishable bread.

Remember that the Bread of Heaven is broken so that the eyes of faith may be opened and you will not remain unbelieving.

Remember that the Bread of Heaven makes you a companion of Jesus and seats you at the Father's table, from which none of your brothers and sisters is excluded.

Remember that the Bread of Heaven enables you to live in intimacy with your God and in solidarity with your brothers and sisters.

Remember that the Bread of Heaven was broken on the cross so that you might eat it, and was given generously for the salvation of all.

Remember that the Bread of Heaven is multiplied when you share it.

Remember that the Bread of Heaven is blessed, broken with his hands wounded for love, and served to you by the same risen Lord.

Remember! Remember! Never forget!

CATECHISTS

Catechists are given one mission in the Church: to make others believe in the Gospel. Seeing you, seeing what you do, how you act, what you say, how you feel, how you love: that they may believe in the Gospel.

We cannot remain isolated; we cannot remain in the parish or in the school. Catechists, take to the streets! Catechize, search, knock on doors—knock on hearts.

As catechists, you well know, through the wisdom gained by being with people weekly, that the desire and need for God is alive in men and women.

Today more than ever it is necessary "to adore in spirit and in truth" (Jn 4:24). That is the indispensable work of the catechist who wants to be rooted in God, who doesn't want to lose courage in the midst of so much turmoil.

Today more than ever it is necessary to adore, thus making possible the closeness [to others] that these times of crisis demand. Only in the contemplation of the mystery of Love that vanquishes distances and comes close, will we discover the strength to resist the temptation to follow from afar, without stopping on the way.

Today more than ever it is necessary to teach our children how to adore, so that our catechesis will truly be an initiation and not just a teaching.

Today more than ever it is necessary to adore so as not to smother ourselves with words, which at times hide the mystery, instead of gifting ourselves with a silence full of admiration. Such silence is quiet before the Word that makes itself so present and close to us.

Today more that ever it is necessary to adore!

In thanking you for your service as catechists, I ask our Eucharistic Lord to renew your apostolic ardor and fervor. May you never grow accustomed to the faces of so many children who do not know Jesus, to the faces of so many youths who drift through life without meaning, to the faces of so many who are excluded. With their families and their elderly, the latter fight for their community, even as their daily passage through our city saddens and challenges us.

More than ever we need your clear vision as catechists in order to see rightly. Allow yourselves to be moved, stopping whenever needed in order to give to our journey the healing rhythm of solidarity. And in this way you will be able to make of the journey an experience of true compassion, the compassion of Jesus, who, far from paralyzing, mobilizes, even pushes one to go out with more strength, more audacity, to announce, to heal, to liberate (see Lk 4:16–22).

More than ever we need your delicate catechist's heart that allows you to carry, from [the perspective of] your experience of accompaniment, the wisdom of life and of the processes where prudence stands out. [We need your] capacity to comprehend, the art of hoping, the meaning of belonging, in order to take care of the sheep entrusted to us, [guarding them] from the cunning wolves trying to disperse the flock.

More than ever we need you and your catechetical ministry, so that with your creative gestures, you may, as David did, bring music and joy on your journey with God's tired people (see 2 Sam 6:14–15)!

The catechist's heart is subject to this double movement: centripetal and centrifugal (to receive and to give). It is centripetal insofar as receiving the kerygma as a gift; one welcomes it into the center of his or her heart. It is centrifugal insofar as it is announced with an existential necessity: "Woe to me if I do not evangelize" (I Cor 9:16).

CHRISTIAN

We Christians have a starting point, a reference that presents itself to us as light and guide. Christian discernment is precisely Christian because it makes Jesus Christ its axis.

In the life of every Christian, of every disciple, of every catechist, the desert experience cannot be lacking: interior purification, the dark night, the obedience of faith such as our father Abraham lived. But there also is the root of discipleship, of surrender, and the experience of God's people, which allows us to recognize ourselves as their brothers and sisters.

We Christians have a specific contribution to make in our homeland, and you educators ought to be protagonists of a change that cannot be delayed. I invite you to this change and, so that it may come about, I place my trust in you.

Each day we ought to allow Christ to transform us and make us like himself. This means to try to live as Christians, to try to follow Christ, even if we see our limitations and weaknesses. The temptation to leave God aside in order to place ourselves at the center is always at the door, and the experience of sin wounds our Christian life, our being children of God.

CHRISTMAS

He is at the door of your heart and he is calling you. God is coming. Christmas reminds us that he came once and that he will come again, and he invites us to receive him every day.

Christmas is finding Jesus. On this holy night, we are invited to ask ourselves how we can encounter Jesus. Am I disposed to encounter Jesus, or do I allow myself to go through life as if everything has already been determined? No, Jesus is knocking on your heart. Jesus is telling you the same thing the angel told the shepherds: A Redeemer has been born for you. He simply asks that you listen to him, or more, he asks that you look for him. Today he invites us to search for him.

CHURCH

In these three readings I see that there is something in common: it is movement. In the first reading, the movement on the journey; in the second reading, movement in building up the Church; in the third reading, the Gospel, movement in confessing faith. Walking, building, confessing.

To walk. Our life is a journey, and when we stop walking something is wrong. We walk always in the presence of the Lord, by the light of the Lord, trying to live with that honor that God asked of Abraham, in his promise.

To build. To build the Church. We speak of stones: stones are solid, but [the stones spoken of are] living stones, stones anointed by the Holy Spirit. Build up the Church, the Spouse of Christ, on the cornerstone that is the Lord himself. With every movement in our life, let us build!

To confess. We can walk as much as we want, we can build many things, but if we do not confess Jesus Christ, something is not right. In the end we would be a charitable NGO, but not the Church, Spouse of the Lord. When one doesn't walk, one stands still. What happens when one does not build on stones? The same thing that happens to children when they build sand castles on the beach. Everything falls down. There is no solidity. When Jesus Christ is not confessed, I recall what Leon

Bloy said: "Whoever does not pray to the Lord, prays to the devil." When one doesn't confess Jesus Christ, one confesses the worldliness of the devil, the worldliness of the demon.

To walk, to build, to confess. But it's not that easy, because in walking, in building, in confessing, sometimes there are earthquakes, movements that are not properly part of the journey—they are movements that make us retreat.

My wish is that all of us, after these days of grace, will have the courage, yes, the courage, to walk in the presence of the Lord, with the Lord's Cross; to build the Church on the Lord's blood, which was poured out on the Cross; and to profess the one glory: Christ crucified. And in this way, the Church will go forward.

My prayer for all of us is that the Holy Spirit, through the intercession of the Blessed Virgin Mary, our Mother, will grant us this grace: to walk, to build, to confess Jesus Christ crucified. Amen.[*]

_____

* From the first homily of Pope Francis, March 14, 2013.

CITY

God lives in the city and the Church lives in the city. Mission does not resist having to learn from the city—from its cultures and its changes—while, at the same time, we go out to preach the Gospel to the city. And this is a fruit of the same Gospel, which interacts with the terrain on which it falls like a seed. Not only is the modern city a challenge, but all cities, all cultures, all mentalities, and all human hearts have been, are, and will be challenged.

Our God, who lives in the city and involves himself in its daily life, does not discriminate, nor does he relativize. His truth is that of the encounter that discovers faces—and each face is unique. To include people with faces and personal names does not imply relativizing values or justifying anti-values. Rather, to refrain from discriminating and relativizing implies having the fortitude to accompany processes and having the patience of the fermenting agent that aids growth. The truth of the one who accompanies is that of showing paths farther ahead rather than judging the past.

This city abandons its children, politely calling them "street children." It abandons them and throws them into the street. This city doesn't cry. And because this city doesn't know how to cry, it isn't a mother. Today[*] we come here to cry so that this city may become a mother, so that instead of killing, this city may learn to give birth, so that it may be a promise of life.

Being pilgrims in our city means not being comfortable, but being open to life. It means paying attention to what happens in our heart, like a Good Samaritan before the difficult reality so many of our brothers and sisters must face.

Sow hope in the city. I ask you: sow hope in the city, that you may be channels, instruments, so that the Holy Spirit may introduce each man, each woman, each boy, each girl into the mystery of God. Our city needs this. Our neighborhoods need this. Our families need this. Our workplaces need this. We all need this.

---

* Homily of December 30, 2009, for the fifth anniversary of the tragedy of the massive fire at the Cromagnon nightclub in Buenos Aires, in which 194 people died.

COMMUNICATOR

Being a communicator is not merely a function. It goes beyond that. It roots itself in that sphere of interiority where the project of life gestates and unfolds itself along the path of existence. Every man and woman is a communicator, but you are even more so by your special dedication.*

---

* Address to a group of journalists, April 6, 2006.

To communicate is the action of putting something in common; human communication involves establishing bonds between people. Social communication begins with concrete persons and is directed at other concrete persons. In establishing relationships between them, a social knitting is formed on which the life of the community is constructed.

The great challenge of communicators, who from day to day go out to search for the truth so as to later tell it to others, is to remember for themselves and concretize in their work the reality that the true, the good, and the beautiful are inseparable.

CROSS

Christian triumph is always a cross, but a cross as a banner of victory.

The resurrection is not understood without the cross. In the cross is the story of the world: grace and sin, mercy and repentance, good and evil, time and eternity.

The cross only has meaning for us who believe in eternal life.

For the one who does not believe in eternal life, who believes only that life ends here and is created here, and who lives in this manner, the cross has no meaning. Such a person does not understand the cross. It is no more than a decoration to wear because it is stylish, nothing more; it is not the triumph of God's salvation among us.

The cross is the search for the love of God that comes out of himself in order to call us to love him: love with Love.

DEATH

Dying is precisely throwing oneself into those hands [of God]. It is a new beginning . . . yes and no, because those hands have accompanied us our entire life, though at times we haven't realized it. But [death] is the revelation of those hands that have been accompanying us, that have never left us, and that now receive us.

DIVESTING ONESELF

Divest yourself of all pretension. Divest yourself of all ephemeral illusion and go to the essential, to what promises you life, to what gives you dignity. Lower yourself; do not be afraid of humility; do not fear meekness. Today we are told that the <u>more you put your nose in the air, the more important you are</u>. <u>No</u>. Today we are told that if you appear to be <u>vain</u> enough, you will have more strength. No, that is not the way things are. Today we are told that the more you scream and fight, the more discord you sow, the better it is for you. No, that is not the case. Lower yourself, use meekness. Listen, live with others. Recognize your dignity and that of others. Love and allow yourself to be loved.

EDUCATION

An educational community is a small church, greater than the family and smaller than the diocesan Church. In [this educational community] one lives and lives with. In it we are on pilgrimage toward eternity as sons and daughters.

To offer some knowledge, propose some values, awaken some possibilities, and share one's faith are works that can have only one motive: trust that those seeds will grow and produce fruit at their time and in their manner. To educate is to invest in and contribute to the present and the future. And the future is driven by hope.

We want to ask forgiveness of children because we don't always take them seriously. We don't always provide the means so that their horizon does not lead to a dead end. We often do not strive to inspire them to greater horizons that will help them value what they have received and have to pass on. [We ask forgiveness] because we often didn't know how to make them dream!

Our schools are called to be true signs, living signs that "what you see is not all that there is," that another world, another country, another society, another school, another family is possible. [Our schools are] called to be institutions where new forms of relationship are cultivated, along with new paths of fraternity, a new respect for the uniqueness of each human being, a greater open-ness and sincerity, and a workplace atmosphere characterized by collaboration, justice, and respect for each person. [In such schools] manipulative relationships, competitions, back door dealings, authoritarianism, and interested favoritism will have no place.

Our work has a goal: to foster something in the students who have been entrusted to us; to foster a change, a growth in wisdom. We desire that, after having passed through our classrooms, our children and young people will have experienced a transformation, and will have more knowledge, new feelings, and, at the same time, attainable ideals.

Our students have the right, above all, not only to their own autonomy and uniqueness, but also to develop socially recognized, proven abilities, in order to bring their desires and their contributions to the real world.

From the objectivity of the truth let us propose open and inspirational ideals and models, without setting in stone the means we have found to be useful, while at the same time developing the necessary means so that children can choose their options. We prefer to form students who are free and responsible, able to question themselves, to decide for themselves, even if they make mistakes along the way, who do not merely imitate our own decisions . . . or our errors.

The neighborhood school contributes actively to form ties, to create identity, to value shared spaces. The school relates families among themselves and with the larger neighborhood community, with institutions, with the "nets" that give form to the life of the city. The school is a point of reference and the heart of the neighborhood for so many families. A school should always be well inserted in its reality and not be just an island attentive only to its internal problems.

The only motive we have for working in the field of education is the hope for a new humanity, according to the divine design. It is the hope that blossoms from Christian wisdom, in which the resurrected Jesus reveals to us the divine heights to which we are called.

Another temptation [in education] is to favor cerebral values over the values of the heart. The temptation is in removing understanding from the place where God our Lord put it.

EUCHARIST

The Gospel marks our course: to sit at the table and allow ourselves to be summoned by the profound gesture of Christ. The blessed bread should be shared. It is the fruit of sacrifice and of work. It is the image of eternal life, which ought to be realized already.

The Eucharist is the great sign of the Lord's ardent desire to nourish us, to give us life, to enter into communion with human beings. That is why it is the sacrament of our faith, the proof of his love. We who have the grace of living in this blessed land, and who know how to discern what is good bread, cannot replace that hunger for the true Bread. . . .

- ❧ We say yes to the Bread of Life—Jesus Christ—and we say no to the substances of death.

- ❧ We say yes to the Bread of Truth, and we say no to the wordiness of empty and banal discourses.

- ❧ We say yes to the Bread of the common good, and we say no to all exclusion and all inequality.

- ❧ We say yes to the Bread of Glory that breaks for us [the bread of] the resurrected Jesus, and we say no to pagan vulgarity that leaves the heart empty.

The Lord has not only the love whereby he gives himself, but also the delicacy of making us participants in the sweet work of love. And in sharing love we become community. Because the Bread creates bonds, it enables us to stay; it enables us to work together to prepare it and then to remain at table talking, to give him thanks.

Only his living bread has the strength to bring the crowd together in such a manner. Only the strength of his death on the cross in order to make himself bread is able to convert crowds into communities. And we ask him:

Lord, give us always this Bread!

We want to be a community that shares the bread that you bless and distribute.

We want to be a community that organizes itself according to your way, so as to permit you to serve and transform us.

We do not want to eat our bread alone: neither the bread of faith nor the bread of work.

We do not want to "dismiss" the crowds, who, when they gather, look for you and desire you, often without even knowing it.

We do not want to resignedly accept the statistics that already write off so many of our brothers and sisters.

We want to be communities who live from the strength which the Eucharist gives, so as to announce—with our lives more than with our words—the truth of the Gospel that is transcendent because it speaks of that which is beyond individualism. It speaks of a Kingdom that is already in our midst when we gather to share bread in your name, Lord.

FACING FEAR

Often, new things make us fearful, including the new things that God brings us, that God asks of us. We are like the apostles in the Gospels: many times we prefer to keep our own certainties, to stand in front of a tomb, thinking of a deceased person, who in the end only lives in historical memory, like the famous people of the past. We are afraid of God's surprises; we are afraid of God's surprises. He always surprises us.

We are, perhaps, often tired, disillusioned, sad; we feel the weight of our sins, and we think we cannot achieve things. Let us not withdraw into ourselves; let us not lose confidence; let us not resign ourselves. There is no situation that God cannot change; there is no sin that he cannot forgive if we open ourselves to him.

The Spirit of the resurrected Christ drives out fear from the apostles' hearts and impels them to come out of the Cenacle to proclaim the Gospel. Let us also have more courage so as to witness to our faith in the resurrected Christ! We ought not to fear being Christians and living like Christians! We ought to have this courage and go and announce the resurrected Christ, because he is our peace. He has made peace with his love, with his forgiveness, with his mercy.

FAITH

How beautiful in our life is this reality of faith: the mercy of God. The love God has for us is so great, so profound. It is a love that does not diminish; it is a love that always grasps our hand and holds us, raises us, guides us.

Our faith is revolutionary, it is built on itself. It is a spirited faith, but not with the fighting spirit for just any skirmish, but for a project discerned under the guidance of the Spirit for a greater service to the Church and the world. And, on the other hand, the potential liberator comes to it not from ideologies, but precisely from his contact with the holy.

Faith must be asked for. May God help us to be persistent beggars, continuously imploring God and his saints. To deny that the prayer of petition is by its nature superior to other prayers is the most subtle pride. It is only when we are persistent beggars that we recognize ourselves as creatures. When we don't kneel before the faith of the humble, when we don't allow ourselves to be taught, and when we don't know how to ask, then we begin to say that what saves is pure faith, an empty faith, but a faith dry of all religion, of all piety.

By definition faith, hope, and charity constitute fundamental attitudes that raise us higher, an ecstasy of man toward God. They truly transcend us. They make us go beyond and transcend ourselves.

The faith of the disciple holds fast and grows in the encounter with the living Jesus, who touches every area of life. The disciple is nourished in the experience of facing the Gospel so as to live it as good news that illuminates our daily journey.

Unfortunately, often faith in Jesus's resurrection has been weakened and doubts have been insinuated among believers. In a certain sense, a faith "of rose water,"* we might say, is not a strong faith. And this is due to superficiality, at times because of indifference, occupied in a thousand things considered more important than faith, that is, by a merely horizontal vision of life.

---

* That is, a faith without substance. —Trans.

FAMILY

A family that does not respect nor take care of its grandparents, who are that family's living memory, is a fractured family. But a family and a people that do remember them are a family and a people of the future.

The family is a necessary condition so that a person becomes aware of and values his or her own dignity. In the family we are loved as we are; our happiness and our vocation are valued more than other interests.

FORGIVENESS

Have you thought about God's patience, the patience that he has for each one of us? That is his mercy. He always has patience, patience with us. He understands us, he waits for us, he does not tire of forgiving us if we know how to return to him with a contrite heart. "Great is your mercy, O LORD," says the psalm (119:156).

Let us not forget this: God never tires of forgiving. Never. "And, Father, what is the problem?"

The problem is *we* get tired, we don't want it, we get tired of asking forgiveness. God never tires of forgiving, but sometimes we get tired of asking forgiveness. May we never weary of it, may we never weary of asking forgiveness. God is a loving Father who always forgives, who has a merciful heart for us.

God is patient with us because he loves us, and he who loves understands, hopes, gives confidence, does not abandon, doesn't burn bridges, and knows how to forgive. Let us remember in our Christian life: God always waits for us, even when we have separated ourselves from him. He is never far away, and if we return to him, he is ready to embrace us.

Dearest brothers and sisters, let us allow ourselves to be enveloped in God's mercy. Let us trust in his patience, for he always gives us his time. May we have the courage to return home, to live in the wounds of God's love, allowing him to love us and encountering his mercy in the sacraments. We will feel his tenderness, which is so beautiful. We will feel his embrace, and we too will be more capable of mercy, patience, forgiveness, and love.

It isn't easy to entrust oneself to God's mercy, because it is an incomprehensible abyss, but we must. "Oh, Father, if you knew about my life, you would not speak to me that way." "Why? What have you done?" "Oh, Father! I have sinned so much." "Even more, then, go to Jesus! He likes it when [people] tell him these things." He forgets, he has a great capacity for forgetting, a very special one. He forgets, he kisses you, he hugs you and solemnly tells you, "Neither do I condemn you. Go your way, and from now on do not sin again" (Jn 8:11). He gives you only that advice. After a month, we may find ourselves in the same condition. . . . Let us return to the Lord. The Lord never tires of forgiving, never! We are the ones who tire of asking for forgiveness. And we ask for the grace to never tire of asking for forgiveness, because he never tires of forgiving. Let us ask for this grace.

FRAGILITY

Something "fragile" is "that which is easily broken to pieces." The Gospel image we contemplate is the Lord who "is broken into little pieces" of bread and surrenders himself. In the broken bread—so fragile—the secret of life is hidden: the life of each person, of each family, of the entire homeland.

In the Lord's loving fragility there is good news, a message of hope for us. The generous and total surrender that Jesus desired to make so as to save us remains preserved in the Eucharist, safe from all attempts by human beings to manipulate it.

Against the fragmentation that comes from selfishness, we ask for the grace of loving fragility that comes from surrender.

Against the fragmentation that makes us fearful and aggressive, we ask the grace to be like the bread that is broken so as to provide for all. And not just for the sake of providing, but also for the joy of sharing and exchanging it with one another.

Against the fragmentation of isolation and immersion in one's own interests, we ask for the grace to be whole, each one at his post, fighting for everyone, for the common good.

Against the fragmentation that comes from skepticism and distrust, we ask the Lord for the grace of faith and hope that brings us to spend and consume ourselves, trusting in him and in our brothers and sisters.

Our vocation would not be complete if it excluded our mud, our falls, our brokenness, our daily struggles: it is here that the life of Jesus is manifested and becomes a saving message. Thanks to our vocation, we discover the pains of our brother and sister as our own.

Holiness—to be holy—is not something belonging to a bygone era. Today, too, there are men and women who place themselves in fragile situations in order to care for the fragility of others and revive them. And more so the fragility of life.

Jesus himself pointed out the way for us. He who was strong made himself weak; he who was rich made himself poor; he who was great made himself small. He made himself fragile, so as to accompany our daily fragility with his fragility taken up to the cross.

FRANCIS

Some didn't know why the Bishop of Rome wanted to call himself Francis. Some thought of Francis Xavier, Francis de Sales, or Francis of Assisi. I will tell you the story. During the elections, I had at my side the archbishop emeritus of São Paolo, Brazil, who is also the prefect emeritus of the Congregation for the Clergy, Cardinal Claudio Hummes: a great friend, a great friend. When things got a bit "dangerous," he comforted me. And when the votes reached two-thirds, the customary applause began because I had been elected. And Cardinal Claudio hugged me, kissed me, and said to me: "Do not forget the poor." And this word entered here: the poor, the poor. Immediately, in relation to the poor, I thought of Francis of Assisi. Then, while the scrutiny proceeded until all the votes were finished, I thought of the wars. Francis is also the man of peace. In this way, the name entered my heart: Francis of Assisi. For me he is the man of the poor, the man of peace, the man who loves and who cares for creation. Now our relationship with creation is not so good, is it? He is the man who gives this spirit of peace, the poor man. Oh, how I would like a Church that is poor and is for the poor!

HOLY SPIRIT

The Spirit is the one who drives us, who also guides us on the path toward all those on the fringe of human life: where many people do not know God, where there is injustice, pain, loneliness, life without meaning. We need to evangelize in these areas of pressing need,* but the Spirit has to take us there.

---

* Literally, "existential peripheries." —Trans.

When the Spirit of Truth comes, he will introduce you to all Truth. That is the first of the many works that the Spirit does in us: he places us within the Mystery of God. He introduces us into the Mystery of God. None of us can even say the name of Jesus with faith unless the Holy Spirit impels us.

Lead your brothers and sisters to enter the Mystery of God. Not you, the Holy Spirit. But you can be the conduit of the Holy Spirit so that this society, all of it, our brothers and sisters who received holy Baptism—the majority who have the seal of the Spirit, the Unction of the Spirit— may recognize the path to the Mystery of God.

HOMELAND

Today, as we pray for our homeland, we ask for the grace of knowing how to take care of our elderly and our children, so that pragmatism, consumerism, and hedonism do not treat them as something to be used and thrown away by our current selfish [society]. May the homeland feel more like a homeland, recognizing their dignity and promoting their rights.

Jesus Christ, Lord of history, give us the grace to know how to enjoy our fellowship and humble friendship that motivate us to build together, because we feel ourselves to be sons and daughters of your Father and our Father. Awaken our sluggish hearts from our rivalries and pettiness before it is too late. May we not listen with pride and ambition to the fears that make us empty and hollow, but may we carry the gentle yoke of sharing without dominating because it is a duty of justice, with our brothers, with ourselves, and with you.

In these very difficult times of our homeland, in which the lowering of morals appears to weaken everything, it does us good to raise our eyes to the Eucharist and remind ourselves of the hope to which we have been called. We are invited to live in communion with Jesus.

We have the responsibility for the wounded, who are the nation and its people. Today begins a new stage in our homeland, marked most profoundly by fragility: the fragility of our poorest and most excluded brothers and sisters, the fragility of our institutions, the fragility of our social ties. . . . We must take care of the fragility of our wounded people! We must take care of the fragility of our homeland.*

---

* Homily for "Day of the Homeland," May 25, 2003.

HOPE

Hope presents itself, first of all, as the capacity to weigh everything and to keep the best of each thing—that is, to discern. But that discernment is not blind or improvised; it is realized on the basis of a series of presuppositions and ordered to some aspects of an ethical and spiritual character. This implies asking ourselves what is good, what we desire, where we wish to go. This includes a return to values that support themselves in a paradigm. Definitely, hope ties itself strongly to faith. In that way hope sees farther, opens new horizons, invites to greater depths.

Christian hope, in that way, awakens and empowers energies that were perhaps buried in our past—personal or collective—the grateful memory of joyful and happy moments, passion perhaps forgotten by truth and justice, the sparks of plenty that love has produced in our path.

Christian hope is not, therefore, a "spiritual consolation," a distraction from the serious works that require our attention. It is a dynamic that frees us from all determinism and from every obstacle so as to construct a world of liberty, to liberate that history from the chains of selfishness, inertia, and injustice.

In the authenticity of our hope we know how to discover, in daily life, the great or small reasons to recognize the gifts of God, to celebrate life, to emerge from the chain of "ought" and "have to" so as to unfold the joy of being seeds of a new creation.

Hope liberates us from that centripetal force that carries people today to live in isolation in big cities, waiting for a delivery person and connected only virtually. The believer who looks with the light of hope fights the temptation of not seeing the gift, or of living walled inside the bastions of one's own nostalgia or curiosity. Hope's gaze is not the eager glance "to see what happened today" as news reporters tell.

Hope is the virtue of what is arduous but possible, that which invites. Yes, it is to never lower one's arms, not in a merely arbitrary way, but by finding the best way of keeping them busy, of doing something real and concrete.

HUMILITY

Humility reveals, to the smallness of our human self-awareness, its power. In effect, however, when we are more conscious of both our gifts and limitations, we will be more free of the blindness of pride.

JESUS CHRIST

All encounters with Jesus change our hearts and make us bold and daring, so as to defend what we have received, what cannot be negotiated. Up to the point where the apostles could not negotiate, they all died as martyrs and sealed with their life the certainty of this encounter.

Jesus is someone great, he is someone who changes our life, purifies our heart, and enlarges it to be magnanimous, with wide horizons, with room for everyone.

Jesus, who proclaims how God expresses himself in the limitations of his incarnation, wanted to share human life, and this is redemption. What saved us was not only the "death and resurrection of Christ," but also Christ incarnate, his birth, fasting, preaching, healing, dying, and rising.

Jesus always looks at the edge of the path and calls us. This attitude is proper to Jesus: looking at those who are on the edge of the most difficult moments of existence, on the edge of the path of existence, and calling them.

Jesus Christ is the way of the humility of God, of the humiliation of God. He lowered himself. Being God, he lowered himself to be one like us. He did not only share our life, but he also carried our sins so as to conquer the death of sin with his death and resurrection.

Jesus entered in patience. And yet how we become impatient; with what arrogance we sometimes expect to be treated as just, when the just one was treated as a sinner.

We are all moved when someone wants to be with us simply because they love us. Jesus is also moved when people want to stay with him. Simple people intuit that this is the most profound [part] of God's heart: Jesus is God with us, the God who came to remain in our history: "I am with you always, to the end of the age" (Mt 28:20).

Our life invites us to have a heart that sees in the way that Jesus sees our heart. He entered into it, healed so many wounds, and cured so many pains. Have a heart that sees, not a bad heart that does evil to others, harms them, such as that of the brigand. Someone may say to me: "Father, I never went out with a stick to hit a neighbor." But did you hit your neighbor with your tongue? How many times do we strike those closest to us with our tongue? And that is why we do not look at our neighbor with our heart.

Jesus rests in his most profound center: that of feeling himself to be the beloved Son, joined to those same small ones who received from his hands the Father's love. That love relieves, softens, nourishes, and in Jesus life ceases to be a burden. The fraternal solidarity that gives life removes the burden and the disproportionate weight with which our own presumption and obstinacy choke the soul.

Our Lord Jesus Christ breaks into our history—marked by vulnerability—with an unstoppable dynamism, full of strength and courage. That is the kerygma, the nucleus of our preaching: the definitive proclamation of that entrance of Jesus Christ incarnate, who died and rose, into our history.

Accept then that resurrected Jesus in your life; welcome him with trust, as a friend. He is the Life! If until now you have been far from him, take a small step: he will welcome you with open arms. If you are indifferent, take a risk: you will not be misled. If it seems difficult to follow him, do not fear, but trust him, secure in the knowledge that he is close to you, he is with you, and he will give you the peace you seek and the strength to live as he wishes.

JOY

Joy is made manifest when we put our hand to the plow, bear fruit, and do everything that Jesus tells us to do (see Jn 2:5).

A fuller life is a happier life. Everything we can imagine as part of a "happy life" includes my peers. There is no real and true humanism unless it includes the full affirmation of love as a union between human beings, in the distinct ways in which this union is realized: interpersonal, intimate, social, political, intellectual, etc.

Joyful, committed, renewed in your fervor. . . . Make present that style of missionary Church that knows about fragilities—its own and those of others—and for that reason goes out, embraces, and accompanies.

To express in our life the sacraments we have received [Baptism and the Eucharist]: see here, beloved brothers and sisters, our daily commitment, but also our daily joy. This is the joy of feeling oneself to be an instrument of the grace of Christ, like branches of the vine that is Christ himself, animated by the vitality of his Spirit.

LENT

At this beginning of Lent, blessed will these forty days be if they train our hearts in the permanent attitude of breaking and sharing our daily bread with those most in need. Our fasting cannot be only an occasional gift, but an invitation to grow in the freedom through which we experience that the one who has more is not happier, but that the happier person is the one who shares more because he or she has entered into the dynamic of God's gratuitous love.

We would be ashes, but ashes that carry the signs of the love we have given while on earth. Therefore Lent, framed with this principle, speaks to us of the love with which we were created, and the love that we must carry and leave behind at the end.

Let our fasting come from concrete solidarity, as a visible manifestation of the love of Christ in our life. In this way our fasting has meaning as a prophetic gesture and an efficacious action. In this way our fasting makes sense so that others will not have to fast. To fast is to love.

Leave behind some entertainment, and place yourself in silent prayer. Do some penance so as to accompany your people in their pain. Deprive yourself of something and give it away so that others may have nourishment, medicine, whatever they need. These people are our brothers and sisters. And my brother is there on the fringe of my existence; my brother is suffering and I cannot pretend I don't see.

Strip yourself of selfishness and look around to see what you can give up so as to help the one who needs alms. If you do this during Lent, your heart will look to higher things, and you will be greatly surprised at the end.

"Rend your hearts and not your clothing. Return to the LORD, your God" (Joel 2:13). That is to say, this is Lent's theme: Let us allow ourselves to be reconciled with God; it is Jesus who reconciles us! Let us give Jesus space so that he can reconcile us, and we will return to the Lord with all our heart.

Lent is not about being sad, wearing a listless face (as Jesus says in the Gospel). Instead it is for gazing at that horizon of love and opening our hearts, allowing that these desires spring from something greater.

Frequent meditation on the Word of God and the voluntary privations of Christians during this time of grace are meant not only to bear fruit in the purity of their heart, but also to lead to rich and varied works of mercy toward our most needy brothers and sisters.

LIFE

Take care of the elderly. Take care of the lives of the elderly because that is how to be a family! And do not act in such a way that the elderly are "put away" and unappreciated.

Take care of children. Teach them to grow well so that they may be shoots full of life, who bring forth flowers and fruits in life.

Take care of life, be astute. Take care of lives that are defenseless, that are small and are growing. And, as the good family that we are, take care of the life that is about to end. When people forget to care for their children and their elderly, they began to be a people in decline, a sad people.

God invites us to Life: he brought us here; he has invited us. None of us owns the house of Life; no one has the key. He invites us because he is Life. He makes us participate in his greatness, his beauty, his goodness, his Truth that is Life.

God wants life. He made it. The Bible says that when God made us, he made us in his image and likeness. We are his family; we have his face; we are like him. And the life that he gave us, that he breathed into us, is the one we announce, the one we carry to homes as we go announcing life to people, the way of life.

LISTENING

How many problems we would prevent in our lives if we learned how to listen, if we learned to listen to each other. Listening to someone is to show some interest in that person's life, in his or her heart, and not to pass by as if that person did not matter.

What prevents us from listening? Wanting to impose what I feel, what I believe, what I want. It is to want . . . to dominate or disregard the other or, simply, to be so centered on oneself that the other person does not interest me. So we carry on as if we were blotting the other from our view, as if we were the center of the world. We don't let the other person in.

LOVE

Today, on this day, Jesus invites us to see the fragility of the men and women of our town. Each one has his or her own frailties, and we, who come to God's resting place, are invited to look at the frailties produced by sad, painful stories that rend the heart. He says to us: "Come closer. Take upon yourself the weakness of your brother and sister." And when we want to give someone a tongue lashing, or when we have bad thoughts, we need to remember that the other person is fragile and wounded, and that we could be in his or her place. For that reason treat others as you would want to be treated.

The closeness of the risen Lord, who walks—unrecognized—with the least of the brethren, who awakens the compassion of the Good Samaritan in so many hearts, is the only thing that enflames in so many hearts the fire of the first charity, to return to society with the lasting enthusiasm that the Emmaus disciples had, and to go out and proclaim the Good News of the Gospel.

The one who has means, who has authority, should use them to serve: nothing else matters. Jesus, who is God and man, always has open hands, giving of himself to others. That is why he asks us not to be selfish, because the selfish person has his hands closed, always grasping for himself.

The worst thing that can happen to us is to be without love, so as to look out only for our self-interest. Mary is the woman of love. Without love, there is no room for life. Without love there is selfishness and one turns in on oneself so as to coddle oneself. Today we ask Mary for love so as to care for life. Love and courage!

Let us allow ourselves to be renewed by God's mercy; let us allow the power of his love to transform our lives. Let us make ourselves instruments of this mercy, channels through which God can irrigate the land, guard all creation, and make justice and peace flourish.

MARY

As mother, Mary brings us to encounter the resurrected Jesus, who gives us the courage to go forward and accompanies us magnani-mously on the path of life.

The Virgin Mother, who "treasured all these things in her heart" (Lk 2:51), will show us the grace of remembering. Let us know how to ask her for this grace with humility. She will know how to speak to us in a maternal way, in the language of our parents, the one we learned to babble in during our early years. May we never miss the affection and tenderness of Mary, who whispers in our ear the Word of God in that language.

Here, together with the Mother of Jesus, we come to rest, to entrust others' lives to Mary, the life that many were carrying in silence and prayer along the journey during the pilgrimage. Here the simple and believing people of our country were also growing in something so characteristic of this place: solidarity and fraternity. And in this manner, of encounter and silence, our Mother built this sanctuary: this is the house of Argentinians. Here our homeland grew with the Virgin; here our homeland has her mother.[*]

From deep within her heart, the Virgin has taken care of this country (our homeland),

---

[*] Homily at the Basilica of Our Lady of Luján, May 8, 2010.

beginning from the most poor, those ignored by those who have enough . . . but here they are taken into account. Thus the Virgin's sons and daughters of this land never lack the protection of our Mother.

We ask Mary to keep us safe from the plagues of disunity and contempt: they are the sour fruits of sad hearts. We ask our Mother, Cause of Our Joy—as she is called in one of our most beautiful litanies—to help us taste the Bread of the Covenant, the Body of her Son, so as to keep us united in the faith, cohesive in fidelity, united in the same.

Mary, sealed and anointed by the Holy Spirit, overflows in consolation and praises the Lord. She celebrates God's great deeds throughout history (see Lk 1:46–55). In her painful silence at the foot of the cross, in the painful interior peace of her forbearance, she keeps dwelling on God's history of salvation; for her that is a basis of hope.

Mary is the woman who receives and accompanies life . . . until the end; with all the problems that can possibly arise and all the joys that life also gives. Mary is the woman who, on a day like today, received life and accompanied it until its fulfillment. She still has not completed this task, because she continues to accompany us in the life of the Church so we may move forward. Mary is the woman of silence, of patience, who bears pain, faces difficulties, and knows how to be profoundly happy with the joys of her Son.

MISSION

We need to come out of ourselves, from a tired and apathetic way of living faith, from the temptation of closing ourselves in our own schemes that ultimately close the horizon of God's creative action. God came out of himself to come among us. He pitched his tent among us through his mercy that saves us and gives us hope. If we wish to follow him and remain with him, we too should not be content with remaining in the pen with the ninety-nine sheep. We ought "to go out," to search with him for the lost sheep, the one who is most distant. Remember well: come out of yourselves, like Jesus, like God came out of himself in Jesus, and Jesus came out of himself for us all.

How I wish that the Lord would make us understand and feel that evangelization "is not an optional contribution for the Church. It is the duty incumbent on her by the command of the Lord Jesus, so that people can believe and be saved. This message is indeed necessary. It is unique. It cannot be replaced. It does not permit either indifference, syncretism, or accommodation. It is a question of people's salvation. It is the beauty of the revelation that it represents. It brings with it a wisdom that is not of this world. It is able to stir up by itself faith—faith that rests on the power of God" (Paul VI, *Evangelii Nuntiandi*, no. 5).

We do not have the right to be indifferent and to love ourselves. How I love myself! No, we do not have that right. We need to go out and proclaim that 2,000 years ago, there was a man who wanted to re-establish the earthly paradise, and he came for that reason. To restore all things.

We need to come out of our shell and tell others that Jesus lives, that Jesus lives for him, for her, and to tell them this with joy . . . even though one may at times seem crazy. Saint Paul says that the message of the Gospel is foolishness. Our lifetime is not enough to surrender and announce this: that Jesus has restored life. We have to go to sow hope; we have to go into the streets. We have to go out to search.

The first thing that the Virgin Mary did when she received the Good News in her womb was to go out, running to be of service. Let us go out running to be of service, in that we believe in the Good News and we want to give it to others. Let this be our conversion: the Good News of Christ yesterday, today, and always

We come because we need this place* of trust and rest. We come to tell the Virgin how our life is going, and we receive her glance that encourages us to follow the way. This is not usually publicized, but it is what the children live with much faith, and there are many here who have found their place of encounter and blessing. We come here because we need to continue to trust and nourish what is most ours, what gives meaning to our lives.

We don't want to be that fearful Church that is locked in the cenacle. We want to be the Church in solidarity that encourages itself to go down from Jerusalem to Jericho, without making detours; the Church that encourages itself to come closer to the poorest of the poor to heal them and to receive them.

---

* The Basilica of Our Lady of Luján.

The proposal of a pastoral missionary spirit comes from the need of a new relationship with those who are "outside," that is to say, the non-believers, the distant, the non-practicing, the new cultures, etc., that constitute the most needed area of mission. Such men and women often share the same celebrations, live in the same neighborhoods, work in the same place, and walk in the same city.

MISSIONARIES

In our work of evangelization God asks us to accompany a people that walks in faith. That is why the Lord gives us faces, stories, and searches. . . . And he always makes us remember well that the child, teenager, and adult whom God puts in our path are not vessels we must fill with contents or people we must conquer. The Lord already lives in their hearts, since he always goes before us.

Every encounter with Jesus makes us missionaries, because we are founded on rock and not on the sands of ideologies.

Today more than ever we need your presence in those places where you can be light and joy for so many brothers and sisters who do not realize that God is a Father who loves them with tenderness.

Today more than ever we need your presence so that many families may find in the transcendent love of Christ a new and greater dimension than human love.

Your service to proclaim Christ, being his witnesses in daily life, is to experience and to concretely renew the Baptism that we have received in him, and to convert them into disciples and missionaries of the Word.

NEIGHBOR

Each and every one of us must become a neighbor like the Samaritan. We are all sinful like the Samaritan. But we are asked to come closer, to touch the pain and misery, to touch the injustice, to touch the hidden cries and the loneliness of the elderly, to become neighbors, to touch the wounds of our brothers and sisters because they are the wounds of Jesus Christ.

OLD AGE

Old age—I like saying this—is the seat of the wisdom of life. The elderly have the wisdom gained through their journey of life, like the elderly Simeon and the elderly Anna in the Temple. And it is precisely such wisdom that allowed them to recognize Jesus. Let us offer this wisdom to youth: like the good wine that gets better with the years, let us offer this wisdom of life. What the German poet[*] said about old age comes to mind: *"Es ist ruhig, das Alter, und fromm"*—"age is the time of tranquility and of prayer." Let us also offer this wisdom to youth.

Our cherished young people: they bring us the joy of faith. They say to us that we must always live the faith with a young heart—a young heart even at seventy or eighty years of age. A young heart. With Christ, one's heart never grows old.

---

[*] Friedrich Hölderlin (1770–1843).

Overcoming
Obstacles

One of the most serious temptations that can separate us from the Lord is the feeling of discouragement.

Another temptation is to want to separate the wheat and the weeds before the [harvest] time. Contemplating salvation history gives us a sense of time, because no human process can be forced.

PRAYER

Intercession isn't for the weak. We don't pray so as to "achieve" something, to stay on good terms with our conscience, or to enjoy a purely aesthetic interior harmony. When we pray, we are struggling for our people. Is this how I pray? Or am I tired and bored? Do I try to avoid getting involved in that mess so that my affairs may be peaceful?

The prayer that pleases God is that which moves from a personal encounter with him to a life consecrated to the service of others. Prayer is an expression of openness, of trust, and of our need for God. Whoever feels self-sufficient, who doesn't pray, pleases himself. Authentic prayer requires transparency, consistency, and authenticity.

PRIESTS

Priests need to be formed to pasture [the flock]. To pasture speaks of fortitude and patience, good humor, constancy, tenderness, and compassion. Shepherding requires time so as to journey with others, like the daily work of a mother who nourishes, and a father who opens paths and guides.

The priesthood is for the faithful, for all men and women who need to be anointed with the mercy and charity of God our Father.

It is not flesh and blood that guides our journey as pastors. Neither human prudence nor one's own interest moves us to go from here to there. It is the Spirit who inspires our actions, doing so for the praise and glory of the Father and for the good of God's faithful people.

It is true that we are called to be rocks, but anointed rocks. Hard as rocks on the outside so as to edify and sustain, to protect the flock and cover it, but not hard or irritable on the inside. On the inside the priest must be like oil in a jar, like a flame in a torch, like wind in a sail, like a crumb of bread.

To anoint we must search diligently and receive very intently the anointing of the Spirit in all the corners of our soul, so that grace can reach its depths, superabundantly, and overflow on others.

We are poor priests in the Great Priest, small shepherds in the Great Shepherd. The grace that passes through our lips and our hands is infinitely greater than what we can imagine. The oil of anointing is what makes us good conductors—conductors who are conducted.

When I say that consolation is an option for life, it must be understood that it is an option for the poor and the small, not for the vain and those who consider themselves great. The pastor who trusts in the Lord and goes out to announce the Gospel without a walking stick or an extra pair of sandals, who follows peace—that stable and constant form of joy—[will experience consolation] wherever the Lord sends it down.

In the name of Jesus, we are sent to preach the truth, to do good to all, and to bring joy to the lives of our people. The mission unfolds simultaneously in these three areas. In the first two it is clear: all proclamation of the Gospel is always translated into some concrete gesture of teaching, of mercy, and of justice.

As priests we participate in the same mission the Father entrusted to his Son. Because of that, in every Chrism Mass, we come to renew the mission, to rekindle in our hearts the grace of the Spirit of Holiness that our mother the Church communicated to us by the imposition of hands.

THE SAINTS

The saints are like God's ears, one for each of his people's needs. And we, as well, can be saints in this way, being God's ear in our family, in our neighborhood, in the places where we act and work. [Being a saint is] to be a person who hears what people need, not so as to disturb ourselves or to go tell another, but to gather all these cries and bring them to the Lord.

SEARCH

Search for him in a manger, in a tenement—the sign is the same, looking where no one looks.

Don't search in the midst of big city lights.

Don't search in appearances.

Don't search in that pagan framework that is offered to us all the time.

Search in unlikely places, in what surprises you.

Search like the shepherds who were sent to
 look for a newborn lying in a manger.

Search there. Remove the fallen leaves and
 search below them for the buds of life.
 Search in the simplicity, in the littleness.

Motivate yourself to go out to search, but if
you can't, look at her, the Mother who is simple
and full of gentleness. Ask her to take you by the
hand to search for the Child who is not found in
arrogance or pride, but in the simplicity of all
that is love, gentleness, and goodness.

SERVICE

Service is bowing before the need of the other, whom—in my bowing—I discover as my brother in his need. It is the rejection of indifference and of utilitarian egoism. It is to do for others and because of others. Service is a word that arouses the desire for a new social bond that allows us to serve for the Lord's sake, so that later, through many hands, his divine love may descend and build a new humanity, a new mode of life.

Service is not merely an ethical commitment, nor a volunteering of excessive leisure (idleness), nor a utopian postulate. . . . Since our life is a gift, to serve is to be faithful to who we are; it is about that intimate capacity to give what we are, to love without limits.

A Christian heart never goes on vacation. It is always open to serve where there is a need, because it knows that where there is a need there is a right, and these people, because they are our brothers and sisters, have a right to our attention.

STARTING AFRESH
FROM CHRIST

"To start afresh from Christ" is to concretely imitate the Good Teacher, the only one who has the words of eternal life, and to go out a thousand and one times to the byways, searching for people in their most diverse situations.

"To start afresh from Christ" is to look at the Good Teacher, the one who knew how to differentiate himself from the rabbis of his time because his teaching and ministry were not confined to the Temple precincts. Rather, he made himself the Way, because he went out to encounter the life of his people in order to make them partakers of the first fruits of the Kingdom (Lk 9:57, 62).

"To start afresh from Christ" is to guard prayer in the midst of an aggressively pagan culture, so that the soul does not dry up, the heart does not lose its warmth, and one's actions are not beset by fear.

"To start afresh from Christ" is to feel challenged by his word, by his sending us, and not give in to the temptation of minimalism, that is, to be content with only conserving the faith and to be satisfied that someone keeps coming to religion class.

"To start afresh from Christ" entails continuously undertaking the pilgrimage toward the farthest limits, like Abraham. He was a model of the tireless pilgrim, fearless and full of freedom because he trusted in the Lord. The Lord was his strength and his security. That is how Abraham knew not to stop along the way, because he made his journey in the Lord's presence (see Gen 17:1).

"To start afresh from Christ" is to allow oneself to be displaced, not to hold onto what has already been acquired, to security, to the familiar. I go out to encounter souls because only in God is my soul at rest.

"To start afresh from Christ" assumes not being afraid of the byways.

STEWARDSHIP

The vocation to stewardship is not of concern only for us Christians; rather it has an antecedent dimension that is simply human. It belongs to everyone. It is to safeguard all creation, with all its beauty, as the book of Genesis tells us and as Saint Francis shows us. It is to have respect for all of God's creatures and for the environment in which we live.

It is to safeguard people, to be lovingly concerned about everyone, especially children, the elderly, and the most fragile, who often remain on the periphery of our heart.

It is for each one to be concerned about the others in the family: married couples care for one another and then, as parents, care for their children. And, in time, their children will become caretakers of their parents.

It is to live friendships with sincerity, friendships that protect each other in trust, in respect, and in wishing good for the other. Ultimately everything is entrusted to the care of man and woman, and this responsibility involves all of us. Be stewards of God's gifts.

To safeguard means to be vigilant about our feelings, our heart, because from there emerge good and bad intentions: those that build up and those that tear down. We should not be afraid of goodness and, even more so, of tenderness.

WORK

We have dignity because of work, because we are breadwinners, and that makes us hold our heads high. But when work is not primary and profit becomes the essential, so that making money is put first, then the descent into moral degradation begins. And this descent ends in the exploitation of the worker.

YOUTH

Thank you for having shown to people that others can still dream:

Dreams that can enable the youth to walk across the city.

Dreams that can enable one to immerse oneself in the life of the city and say: "This can change."

Dreams that can enable one to touch hearts and say:

"Laugh, the Lord loves you. Love others
   as well."

Dreams that can enable one to proclaim that
   it is worth taking a chance on Jesus.

We need everyone to plant their dreams in society.

We need your utopias. They can be planted in the social fabric and make green again those of us who are living in sadness.

We need the dreams of all to be put in every corner of the city, because your dreams are not only yours: they belong to those who are daring in life. Encourage yourselves to dream.

Don't fall asleep. Sleeping youth are of little use.

Encourage yourselves to dream. Encourage yourselves to walk and even to risk your life for the Lord.

Jesus walked with you and will continue to walk with you all the way to the Plaza [de Mayo in Buenos Aires].

Jesus has a message that is the greatest of dreams: that we are all brothers and sisters. It is the message of love. You can give it.

Motivate yourselves to plant those dreams. Don't be afraid to dream: if you dream too much you may come crashing back down to reality. Don't worry, but please keep on dreaming! We need your dreams. Do not let go of the dream. Just as I once told you: "Be aware! Don't let anyone put their hands in your pocket and rob you of hope," so today I tell you: "Be careful that no one throws a pail of water on you and douses your dreams."

Do not allow anyone to steal your dreams, not for any proposal that may appear fascinating in the moment, but is over ten minutes later.

Do not allow the dream in your heart to be stolen. God gave you that dream to sow, to reach others, to take a chance for the Lord.

And, believe me, the elderly and the whole city need you to dream, so as to risk your life for Jesus.

ABOUT THE COMPILER

María Gabriela Flores, FSP, is a sister in the congregation of the Daughters of St. Paul. She writes for the digital magazine *Familia Cristiana* in Argentina, and she is the vocation director of the Daughters of St. Paul in Argentina, Paraguay, and Uruguay. Sister Gabriela obtained a degree in journalism from the Catholic University of Argentina.

BOOKS & MEDIA

The Daughters of St. Paul operate book and media centers at
the following addresses. Visit, call or write the one nearest you
today, or find us at www.pauline.org.

CALIFORNIA

3908 Sepulveda Blvd, Culver City, CA 90230   310-397-8676
935 Brewster Avenue, Redwood City, CA 94063   650-369-4230
5945 Balboa Avenue, San Diego, CA 92111   858-565-9181

FLORIDA

145 S.W. 107th Avenue, Miami, FL 33174   305-559-6715

HAWAII

1143 Bishop Street, Honolulu, HI 96813   808-521-2731
Neighbor Islands call: 866-521-2731

ILLINOIS

172 North Michigan Avenue, Chicago, IL 60601   312-346-4228

LOUISIANA

4403 Veterans Memorial Blvd, Metairie, LA 70006   504-887-7631

MASSACHUSETTS

885 Providence Hwy, Dedham, MA 02026   781-326-5385

MISSOURI

9804 Watson Road, St. Louis, MO 63126   314-965-3512

NEW YORK

64 W. 38th Street, New York, NY 10018   212-754-1110

PENNSYLVANIA

Philadelphia—relocating   215-676-9494

SOUTH CAROLINA

243 King Street, Charleston, SC 29401   843-577-0175

VIRGINIA

1025 King Street, Alexandria, VA 22314   703-549-3806

CANADA

3022 Dufferin Street, Toronto, ON M6B 3T5   416-781-9131

¡También somos su fuente para libros,
videos y música en español!